Emblem

Emblem

Richard Hoffman

Barrow Street Press
New York City

Designed by Robert Drummond

The cover image is by Albrecht Dürer, from
Das Narrenschiff by Sebastian Brandt, 1494.

Published by Barrow Street Press
Distributed by:
       Barrow Street
       P.O. Box 1831
       Murray Hill Station
       New York, NY 10156

First Edition

Library of Congress Control Number: 2011936213

ISBN 978-0-9819876-5-1

For Kathi

Words indicate; things are indicated.
But things can also indicate . . .

—*Andrea Alciati*
De Verborum Significatione, *1530*

Against Those Wealthy via Public Mischief

Avarice in check, the country at peace,
does not please everyone. Those who fish

for eels, for example, who know how to slice
one into segments thin as paper dollars

for sushi or paste, must find some way
to roil the placid water and churn the bottom

to be successful. (To stir the muck, religion
makes a good long stick or bogus history

wed to rhetoric.) They know just how.
They have fished for eels a thousand years.

after Alciati's "Emblem 89"

CONTENTS

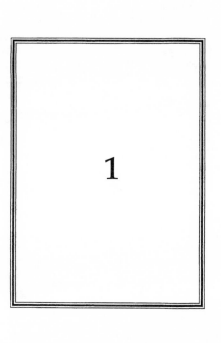

1

Diaspora (Monster)

Someone must have summoned the ancestors,
decided only they could help us out of this one,
because here she comes, irascible and urgent, great-

great-grandmother, saying *Make way, make way!*
in a language only a few here understand.
Although she is terrified, she is willing as ever

to fish you from the pond, post bail, make soup,
even, this time, suffer ridicule and learn
to settle for canned hilarity, eat freeze-dried

produce if that's what it takes; for love of you,
to register at PROGRESS BARGAIN DRIVING SCHOOL
and take the test and drive across deserts

and borders just to find you tangled in your plans,
regrets, and terrors in the city of tomorrow,
everywhere under construction, wooden barricades,

orange DETOUR signs proliferating and compounding
the affront and officious dismissal of one-way streets.
Even now she is stuck in the crosstown jam of

your jackhammered consciousness's flying sparks,
muttering *I'm coming, I'm coming.* See her there?
Do something. Wave your arms. *Over here, over here!*

Husband

I watched the plumber reach down
through the dark water
with his head turned sideways,
feeling for my wife's lost ring,
the index finger of his other hand
admonishing me to wait. I studied his face,
the face of a listening poet, as his other hand
shifted into a mudra—two fingers and thumb,
something like holding a teacup—
that could stand for "confident, quiet waiting."
It was the still gesture of a man
who has heard a bird call, quieting his companion
while he listens for its mate's response, or
a hunter who has just heard a twig snap, or a lover
listening for tires on the gravel drive.
And each time he found something, not the lost ring,
not even nearly the shape of it, he brought it up,
examined it, and placed it in a row
with the other resurrected objects: Wing nut,
wood screw, plastic cap, and something
hard to define, something to look at later.

Procedure

1. Return to your birthplace. But before you do, become as solitary as you can wherever you are.
2. Repeat your name aloud until you understand it only as a sound you make.
3. Set out for your native ground. Travel overland if possible, by water if necessary.
4. Note each obstacle on your way, along with each resistance you experience inside yourself. For example, do you need money? A passport? Another language? Particular items of clothing? A profession of faith or allegiance? Is your lack of resolve an inability to foresee benefit? Is it fear? Procrastination?
5. Immediately upon your arrival, drink the local water. Eat food grown there.
6. Pinch the earth between your thumb and fingers. (If you are right-handed, use your left hand, and vice versa.) Sniff that earth. Note both smell and texture.
7. Attend to the question that will now arise, coherent, in your mind. Be undisturbed until you can clearly speak it.
8. Remain in that place for a length of time roughly equal to the time it took to get there, whispering your question over and over until you hear the music in it.
9. Turn to your left and walk in widening counterclockwise circles.
10. Ask your question of the first person you meet.
11. Listen carefully to the reply.
12. Thank that person with some sort of gift.
13. Heed what you now understand, including what doubts remain.

Ship of Fools

The wynde is up our Nauy is aflote
A bande of Folys a borde is come yet more
Theyr cursed maners and mad I shall nowe note
Whose herte for synne is neyther contryte ne sore

Sebastian Brandt, *Ship of Fools*, 1494
tr. Alexander Barclay, 1874

The Occupation

In the broken city of bread under guard,
our motives remaining subject to revision,
we were modified and sentenced. Period.
We had the right to remain silenced.
We had the right to consider the lilies
in the florist's window. Missionaries
and recruiters taught us history, left us
freedom to choose a god to petition
from the pull-down menu. We went right in,
sat down before a screen. In no time
we were finished and felt relieved.
We liked what we believed we saw.
Licking our sordid fortunes we were sent.
Portions of the future have been prerecorded.

History

A tricornered hat and a flintlock for memory,
glockenspiels marching behind. Watch out
for horseshit and the little birds that peck there.
Speeches. Nobody can recall last week!
Flowers are never a part of the celebration,
nor is dancing. Children must be corrected.
Here come the tanks, the trucks with rockets,
war's worst-off survivors lined up in a row
according to their missing parts. "You are
worse than callous," one man scolds the boy
who points at them, "you're cruel." The flag,
chained to its pole, flaps hard in the wind
and tries to tear itself away. Ka-boom!
First of the fireworks and it isn't even dark yet.

Market Value

A handkerchief, cotton, monogrammed in silk
by inmates, for hardly more than the cost of a meal
for a family of four, a snot-rag of your very own
for purse or pocket, not for tears but for the stench.
Stay away from the vents! You know full well
what to call that smell, and also how to puzzle
over something else instead: What do those clouds
put you in mind of? Do you know what kind
of bird that is? Those cries you'd swear were human
are likely only gulls protesting this our voyage.
Nature is wonderful. Every creature in its own
self-interested domain, competing under one God
almost visible if everyone would raise their voices
louder, louder, everybody! That's much better.

Chartered Streets

The anterior cingulate cortex serves as appestat,
cousin to both conscience and desire. Look:
A couple, handlocked, stand before a storefront
filled with merchandise, entranced; together
they enter the future, dreaming, in a dopamine
jacuzzi, jets full blast and good and hot. The ad,
3-D, before them, offers a telescope of polished brass
fixed on a window, trompe l'oeil, with painted stars:
A library with its tufted leather chairs, mahogany,
oriental carpet, globe, and lifelike sleeping dog.
Take down a volume, read that this very world
is only nifty things to say, or if you don't like poetry,
enjoy a tale about a man who wished his words
to live but turned, instead, his whole life into words.

D.I.Y. Betrayal

We ferried our sullen sirens to the rocks and
handed them the music we composed so long ago
(of crooners' modulated vowels, sustained vibrato,
and jingles for soap and beer that came to occupy
our parents' minds) we had, already, forgotten.
We set the time when they would shed their ever
filthier silence, wired, a lyric bomb, and sing.
It wasn't magic. Even our amnesia was strategic.
O land I love! I was born to your bright promise
and the hard terms of your peace. What I want's
to be your one and only, take me in your arms
and gimme, baby. Gimme wergild of the slain
enslaved, the backpay of the disappeared, gemstones
someone's bound to wear, it may as well be me.

Aftermath

Broken mnemotechnic: An untethered, flat-lined
astronaut still chirping a Springsteen ringtone home.
Hectic traders respond. Tides here are unpredictable.
Let's have some human interest, shall we? Later,
when the panicked have been mollified, we'll count;
till then we'll cybershave one tenth of one percent
off every eagle-faced, toothed coin. Sleep well.
Do not go letting fear awaken secrets marrow knows.
The starry sky and moonmade waves are what to watch.
There is peace. Peace in the intervals. Undulant peace.
Cities, nations, civilizations rise and fall.
Behold, the lesson of the flying fish is superficiality:
From crest to crest across the regularly falling troughs
schools shoot across the open spaces, sometimes
land on deck. Sauteed in butter they're not half bad.

Just War

Your father killed my mother because
her brother shot your grandmother's cousin
for raping his aunt to punish her father
who had swindled his brothers out of land
your great-great-grandmother believed
her father's god had promised her so
what were you doing there worshipping
idols and threatening peace-loving farmers,
descendants of those who were marched
from their homes to wherever they fell
and curled into leathery question marks
that never go away although we try
to answer in the only way that we know how.
You want to know why? That's why.

Landfall

Oh no daddy no big bad no money make moral;
no slow sad mamas wailing moan roll over.
All that hologram-on-hologram tomfoolery,
you'd think we were off to the isle of reward
and not toward Narragonia with sots, profaners,
phonies, gone where the wind untended tends
and schools of thought are born of errors made
en route. You would think we had some idea.
Before we were born and after we are dead
are our coordinates: The chart is blank, our pockets
inside out. By morning we want to be glad and are.
Old buoys ding and dong us in. Gulls laugh.
All passengers on deck. Prepare the dinghies.
Hold your horses, people. Everybody gets there.

Says Who

Says the one who wants things different, not the one who wishes they
        had been.
Says the one who was injured.
Says the one who understands the first addiction's to the future.
Says the one who wondered why so long it changed his body.

Says the man who knows full well he should have spoken long ago.
Says the one who walks in the rain for the sake of walking in the rain.

The one who for her life could not decide to go until this morning,
and the one who removed, relieved, the pistol from his mouth,
chipping a tooth on the sight — they say so too.

And the painter of remembered sunsets and the glare off windows.
And the swimmer turning his head for air.

Says the one who, finished weeping, rakes the ashes.
Says the one who begins to see how things might fit together.
Says the one whose vigil is over, who blows out the candle at sunrise.

The one glad for spring, with the necessary seeds,
the one who explains why the lies were easy to believe,
the one who devotes himself to diagrams and descriptions,
and the one who chooses carefully among the many questions—
all of them say so, all of them.

Says the one who hurries from doorway to doorway.
Says the one who wishes to go on wandering.
Says the one who stands corrected and glad.
Says the one who helped knock down the ruined wall.

Says the one who declined to attend the banquet.
Says the one whose words travel farther than earshot,
who fabricates a name of letters from the alphabet of tears,
who merits the effort to understand,
who trembles, who stumbles, who laughs.

Aphrodisia

Love's language is hyperbole, but whispered,
sibilant similes and promises sotto voce.
It's easy to imagine you've misheard,

the form and content clash, create this weird
distortion like an echo or a tape delay.
Love's language is hyperbole, but whispered.

On which do you place emphasis: The words?
Or the breath? The farfetched or the foreplay?
It's easy to imagine you've misheard

when objectivity has disappeared
and your lover is getting further carried away.
Love's language is hyperbole, but whispered

vows? It's hard to take him at his word,
or hers: Speak up! Proclaim! you want to say.
It's easy to imagine you've misheard,

hard to admit one sharp as you is stirred.
You need to back off, cool down, act blasé.
Love's language is hyperbole, but whispered.
It's easy to imagine you've misheard.

Phototaxis

In a guitar propped in the corner of a dark room in a house where an old musician mourned his wife, music the furthest thing from his mind, a moth lay dormant. It seemed to the man that the many long hours he had spent, day after day, rehearsing in that room, alone, bent over the guitar, along with the countless trips he'd taken to perform his music, had been squandered and would have been better spent with his beloved. He had not gone into that room since she died, his solitude already deeper than he could bear. One day, looking for an old pair of shoes he had somehow mislaid, he entered the room and switched on the overhead light. As he scanned the floor for his lost shoes, the guitar, all by itself it seemed, began to play, soft chords that made the old musician cry out, "Nadia?" He listened. "Nadia?" Nothing—except for a moth batting the ceiling light, punctuating what was otherwise a silence now all the more unbearable, and before he even knew it the guitar was in his hands.

A Man Like That

The enemy hid himself among civilians.
He didn't have even the decency to spare
his parents and his nine-year-old sister.
You see what I mean, a man like that
cares nothing for life, a man like that
is without a conscience, a man like that
can sit there with his family, feet up,
watching TV, eating dates and pistachios,
while missiles crash through the roof
spewing phosphorous on his aged uncle
and cousins, even the baby, without a qualm.
What kind of a man is that? Too cowardly
even to stay alive and watch them burn.
Doesn't he make you angry, a man like that?

Rising

The smoke believes itself a cloud
                    so it rises,
        schooled in billowing, attuned to the beauty
of occlusion and shade, conundrums and accumulation,
                without awareness of the coalescing storm
        soon to extinguish
                its ancestral
                    fire.

Everyone

Columbus thought he had discovered the Indies so he called the people he encountered Indians, but he was wrong; he had discovered the working class.

He took their sage,
not their advice;
it smoldered like rage
but smelled nice.

One of the *Santa Maria*'s crew, avaricious and schooled in flattery, suggested to Columbus that he try calling them "the middle class." They seemed to like that just fine. They smiled. Why not? Sure. Sounds good.

Columbus ordered them given naugahyde and vinyl. Then he watched to see what they would make of it. It stuck to sweaty skin in summer, and in winter it was cold as metal. It cracked, and several cut their buttocks on it.

Eventually they came around, though, when the buffalo were shot to hell, the beaver damned, and the deer and the antelope played out.

Like the real Indians, the real middle class was a world away.

Soon after his return, Columbus was imprisoned for his errors. The King and Queen concurred that these new subjects must forget their names and never know their purpose to the empire. Thus, an edict went forth that there were no classes in the New World because

in the New World, everyone is Middle Class. Everyone.

Apologue

Maybe moths are martyrs
        to the cause of their beloved
            darkness,

kamikaze pilots for the emperor
        of night; or if a candle,
            a light,

is symbol of the truth
        (is, was, and shall be) maybe
            moths fly

from the mouths of liars,
        and if not for a candle
            here or

a candle there, they would
        smother the world with
            dull wings.

Prequel

Carpenters were framing a house across the valley.
Hammers percussed in waves from the surrounding hills.
You took my hand.

Carpenters were framing a house across the valley.
Desolate and lost, from time to time
I could hear their echoing voices.

You took my hand and I pretended ease.
Hammers percussed in waves from the surrounding hills.
You took my hand but I was still untrusting.

Carpenters were framing a house across the valley.
Sometimes I could hear their echoing voices.

You asked what was the matter.
Hammers percussed in waves from the surrounding hills.
You took my hand. I could not tell you,
but I am alive today because you took my hand.

Winter Psalm

Boston snowbound, Logan closed, snowplows
and salt-trucks flashing yellow, drifts
tall as a man some places, visibility poor,
I sit by the window and watch the snow

blow sideways north-northeast, hot cup
in hand, robe over pajamas.
You have made me to seek refuge
and charged me to care for my brothers.

How cruel. That could only be You out there
howling, cracking the trees, burying everything.
What could I possibly want from You
that would not undo the whole world as it is?

2

after Alciati

Emblem 8

Where the God Directs, There One Must Go

If this crossing were another god's,
say that of Pan, or Dionysus, or Shiva,
then we would be enjoined to stroke
the lingam for luck or good weather,
to assure the success of our venture;
but this hill belongs to Mercury,

whose advice can only be had
by performing the ritual: A garland
of blooms from the supplicant's home,
hand-gathered, plaited by one
who longs for the traveler's return,
is placed on the statue's shoulders.

Then with the god's good auspices,
the pilgrim's way is found by wandering:
Every single thing and every relation,
whether plainly seen or only grasped
upon reflection, becomes a metaphor,
and nothing on the path may be disturbed.

Emblem 15

On Wakefulness and Watchfulness

A cock is on the steeple-top
as if to mark the dawn and wake
the sexton from his dream;

in the tower the bell,
recorded, from twin speakers,
seems the voice of a god;

and before the door
stone lions, chiseled into repose,
sneak glances at each other as you pass.

Emblem 37

On Security

To be safe from both the gods and men,
from the cold, the winds, the rain,

dress in the furs of the mice from your barn,
from your own small cache of good days.

This is the way to walk among thieves:
Pocketless, protected by your motley coat,

and able, even so, to catch more mice
to stitch another when this one wears out.

Emblem 50

Deceit against One's Own

Raised from an egg
pirated from its mother
a duckling was taught to beg
bread thrown on the water

and, at first on a string
but soon completely tamed,
it learned to fly, or something
its treacherous teachers named

flying, anyway. When, one day,
as its captors had foreseen,
a great flock rode the flyway
south, in a long, loud, wavy line,

they released their protégé.
Straight up it rose, quacking,
calling out to them, "Brothers, stay;
your tired wings must be aching.

You are foolish to fly so far
to reliably fill your bellies
when just below where we are
are provisions for your families."

Tired and trusting the word
of one who could speak so well
the flock slowed and veered
low to land—and the nets fell.

I'll sum up with an adage:
A naif becomes a knave
when he pretends to knowledge
that he doesn't have.

Emblem 56

On Recklessness

Frat-boy Phaëthon, full of false joy
born of defiant insecurity, big baby
with his bratpack of timid homies
egging him on, takes the patriarchal
chariot for a spin. The palomino
horses of the sun, unreasoning
beasts of pure desire, anticipate
the bit's restraint, but Phaëthon's rein
is weaker than the fury of their fire.
Across the burning earth, disaster:
Star of destruction and death, time
of the wildfires, melanoma, hell
for both the blameless and deserving.
The people's prayer, like smoke
from flaming oil wells, rises: *Zeus,
intercept him. Shoot him down
as promised in the ancient story.*

Emblem 66

On Impulsiveness

Out of habit, fearful, alert
to his surroundings, on the lookout
for his enemies, the bobcat

eats a young deer he has felled.
Look there—in the birch grove!
Another yearling! He's off!

And the dogs devour his kill.

Emblem 86

Against Misers

Septitius, in love with numbers,
suspects his wealth's at risk:
One hacker with his password
and he's wiped out, finished.

His dividends down, his assets
losing value, he counts again,
long crooked finger tracing lines
across and down his spreadsheet,

his heart beats like a rabbit
at the edge of an open field
he will never cross, and time
passes, an uncounted loss.

Emblem 93

On Parasites

A basket of river crabs
for you: Ugly, eyes on stalks,
they are so watchful

for the chance to claw,
pinch, nip, eat any rot
that drifts their way.

Accept them as a gift.
You are what you eat.
You'll love them.

Emblem 107

On Love

Love, a naked youth, smiles gently, approaching.
What has he got there? In one hand flowers,
in the other a fish. Shall we read the meaning

that he rules both land and sea?
For flowers, one must wait for their season,
and to catch a fish means patient waiting too,

as day declines to evening and you doubt your luck
and wonder at the river's mysteries, hoping
down below the worm still wriggles on your hook.

Emblem 116

On Sirens

A wonder
      any mariner
            anywhere in

the vicinity
      of these monsters'
            concupiscent

wiles survives
      to tell the tale;
            no wonder

though that sailors,
      months at sea,
            hear the voices

of their wives
      and (ceaseless sun
            flashing on waves!)

in the cries of
      seals and gulls,
            and in the soft

and long-lashed
      eyes of sea otters,
            feel lust thud

against the hull
      and swoon, fall
            overboard, drown.

Emblem 120

Poverty Hinders Talent

On one hand, wings;
in the other, a stone;

meaning something
like having one foot

on the gas, the other
on the brake, and yet

it's more than that,
you can't just fix it:

Put down the stone
its weight remains,

its print, its shadow,
its obdurate onus

lasts. Survival is first
of prizes, and in that rock

there might be crystals,
jewels, a broken

geode questioning
the use of beauty,

exposed one day,
a poor man's dream.

And toylike wings,
pulsing on a wrist

like a watch with hands
that never move,

pose a riddle too,
about beginnings.

Emblem 152

On Human Life

Now more than ever
weep for our troubles,
Heraclitus: Many
calamities befall us.

You, Democritus,
now more than ever,
laugh: Our life's become
ridiculous.

How long, I wonder,
should I weep with you
over this mess,
my friend Heraclitus?

And how much laughter
dear Democritus,
is too much, and how much
just enough?

3

Mnemosyne's Dummy

Take me from the dark
and onto your knee,
reach in and squeeze my heart;
make my mouth move

until I am almost alive,
the oldest trick in the book:
Your words from my crude
lips, your voice as if mine.

Aspects of the Work

The source of a work and its subject are not the same.
The source of a work and its creator are not the same.
The creator of a work and its subject are not the same.

The power of a work and its impact are not the same.
The power of a work and its intention are not the same.
The intention of a work and its impact are not the same.

The source of a work and its intention are not the same.
The subject of a work and its power are not the same.
The power of a work is not the intention of the work's creator.

When the work's source lies in the intention of its creator,
its impact is restricted to the power of its subject.

When the work's subject is determined by its source,
the power of its impact equals its creator's intention.

Erato

She is beauty itself and sometimes she likes to leave her home
        where sadness is a music
that guides the moon through noctilucent clouds

and venture downhill through the twisting streets
to where the anger is,
        where new regrets are born.

Sometimes she knows the whole night long that come the morning
she will leave with the empty jug on her head
                (steadied by one hand,
the other on her hip for balance)
        and make her way there;
other times, she just up and goes.

Often when she returns
she finds she has lost a gold hoop from one ear,
        which means she will have to go back again.
And because she exists so far beyond our grasp of time,
she has to pace herself, conserve, replenish,

and assent to the unpredictable, particularly love.

Strat and Stompbox

In strum-
me[a]nt, out strum-
pet! Song: Divers
kind of
wonder, attune,
this like that.

I cerebrate
myself and sink,
love aflame
in nescience,
less and less
room, bound-

ing overhear
(say what? [did
you?]) to where's
imp O sing, very
moving, not
impossible, no.

Anamnesis

1.

The care it takes
to be truthful, refusal
upon refusal,
against the tide-pull
of the plausible,
the approximate—

for what? For whom?

Veni, Creator Spiritus,
protect me from haste,
from willfulness,
from forgetfulness,
and the wish to please.

2.

Easy now, easy.

After a good rain,
after dark,

flashlight beam
across cut grass:

Night crawlers glistened,
half out of the earth,

requiring
nuanced touch,
insistent seduction,

to be alive, whole
for use
tomorrow

easy now, easy

one more degree
of untruth and
memory,
muscled as a lip,
will tear, bleed,

easy now, easy.

thumb and fingers,
the way
one holds a pencil
waiting
for the next right word,

easy, easy now

3.

Nostalgia for a flame in a red
glass cup to offset dread;
some human figures carved
or sculpted, ecstatic starved
ascetics, mourners and martyrs
to commemorate the murders
we descend from; organ music
to seize and lengthen the aphasic
spell that is our one defense
against what all this represents.

4.

The synaptic interval, via instrumentation and mathematics,
can be measured, can tell us precisely how long the future takes
to become the past. What a relief! Here in my head the world

abrades and sparks. Still, this kind of understanding is like
those photographs of lightning over the sea or the plains,
exquisite but no longer thrilling because no longer augering

thunder seconds later to disclose how far away the rain is,
how much time we have to take shelter, to gather what we've
brought, to confer with one another whether we will make it.

5.

I guess you had to be there.

6.

Squinting in the sun across
the table at my friend, I can't
remember what it was I meant

to say or why. A house,
says Bachelard, allows us
a dream of safety to dream

a house in which to dream;
also our dream of what was,
what happened, all we call

remembering: Half there
and then, half sun struck here,
dream and dreamer, prey.

7.

What I think
I at least
must do, will
have to do:

Sit silent,
try to see
through wind-shook
trees' and clouds'
reflections:

Inattention
breaks the line,

distractions
spook the fish.

Why This Page Is Blank

The whole poem
    with its delicately
        veined intuition

was on the pale
    underside
        of one leaf

when it turned
    in the sudden ovation
        of windblown maples

before the rain—lost,
    as the first drops fell
        and I ran inside.

Night Walk

The trees appear aluminum in moonlight.
Tomorrow the news will tell what was done.

Shall I ask the marmot for advice?
The quick bats what to do?

The mouse in silver grass, ears cocked
for the whir of wings, notes the owl

has left its branch, while clouds occlude
and then allow the perilous light.

A Fish Story

In those days there were three of us who,
having grown up fishing but stuck now
in the Bronx to go to college, got up
early and headed north, fly rods in hand.

That day we thought we'd try the serpentine
brook that ran along the fairway of the
Country Club, a brook no wider than a sidewalk,
and that's where, off on my own, I saw him:

Across the brook, under a cutbank, holding
his place in the current, a brookie about nine inches.
I backed away and crept downstream,
but not before I noted where he was, precisely,

in relation to a flowering dogwood tree
(I may have added this detail; in any case,
I'm sure that all the rest of this is true.)
I crossed the stream a good ways down

and left my gear there: Rod and reel and
even took off my waders. In a T-shirt, jeans,
and barefoot, I walked slowly till I was about
a dozen yards below that dogwood (or whatever

I had used as a landmark), then lay on my belly
and dangled my left arm in the water. Trout,
I knew, can see only above and to the sides,
but also feel vibrations and disturbances acutely.

I must have taken fifteen, twenty minutes, maybe
longer, to inch my way to him, still there,
and I worried he could hear my pounding heart
where it met the flattened grasses. I stopped.

He swam away a foot or two, ate something tiny,
and returned, precisely, to his previous position.
Soon, an inch at a time, my hand was under him.
I scooped, he flew and landed on the bank,

flapping as if the grass were hot coals. Life
naked, desperate, crying Lord have mercy!
I couldn't grasp it so I slapped it in the water
and never quite believed the story until now.

Cloudy, Chance

He goed, god if he was he seemed sum a way,
knot turning a g(r)ain, the shaper, O ver, O pen

ultimatum: Now you have it, now drips the net, be
great, full, timorousness so last life, must learn

for word, fore sign, and note no thing not a
live, outcrying outloud, until alone you know.

*

Can one (for if one can, then any can) misbe?
Some have come to that, sum of have, of want

fell short and fell hard once and for all from
highnesses, the view from there a horror. Weigh

to go, swung bubbly broken, and wave goodbye.
But Reset's no deity, a flight, and futile too as pyre.

*

No: Grieve among the beasts, here and going
nowhere fast. Last time. Last it, last it out proud

if possible and dour if not and spoken's better,
sum again too quiet out there, whatever common

folly warns, maybe sing; curt syntax of imperatives
on a wing O wing nothing to fear, and one that does.

*

Used to be for sale, slight wear, past perfect
conditional sticks, as is, best offer, free delivery.

Once up on a time, no better no worth, I went
downheaded down to the tale end of earshot there

where birth's all or nothing doing, breath's air's,
not your, in systole, diastole, and a gain began.

*

But now erasure past we widen, praise tiny
as we can, fit thing and that, the quite, the quaint,

catch can since it eludes we know full well,
and oh no not again's a feel we have for more

than one adventing at a time or else abandon
entices in spades and right now. We are lossed.

*

You perhaps. Could be. Never know. Look out.
After all of that I, I, I, I invite you in: Come, yes.

Just us. No body. Or broken through, passed, we
forget, rest, muse; not ours what we make as all's

in our stead. Fixed points fictional means free of,
an open secret, in vita: Of course tomorrow; reply.

Overdose

"The death of the author"

was a suicide

        "A poem should not mean"
(an inter-
diction)
    flarf: A new word,
       "palpable and mute"

"Dumb
as old medallions to the thumb"
        no teethmarks on the coin

caveat emptor

"murk it up a bit" (Lowell)

"Hey!
You've got to hide your love a-way."

And now another
to the list of martyrs, chiseled
on onyx,
        nonrepresentational,
no angel with a book, not even
        a "well-wrought urn"

    stasis encoded,

Watch yourself! (It's impolite to point.)

The author
a cartoon snake that eats its

(sorry) tale,
       stick figure
who draws a door and through it vanishes.

When reading it is considered
        improper to move the lips

or point to the words.

A Good While

I thought of the time I sliced my thumb and how, even there,
      where the nerve endings are most acute, where
          the sensitivity resides
that, touched by each finger in turn, made us human,
      demanded that the ganglions of the head
          learn to cooperate and grow,
and count, and speak, even there with the little cap
      and piece of nail sliced off, for a good while
          I felt nothing
but regret: Oh shit, why'd I go and do that? No pain. Not yet.
      And I thought then maybe a frightened soldier,
          hit by a bullet,
might just die before the pain could start, feeling suddenly
      woozy, sleepy, thinking,
          Shit: I'm hit, blood
pressure dropping fast, dizzy and darkening, maybe
      saying to himself, Oh boy I hope this isn't dying,
          and I prayed, especially
for the sake of my neighbor's son,
      that that is more or less the way it happens.

Dublin Steeple

The church clock's
stopped; its weathervane
stuck. Another year

it will be condominiums,

a satellite dish
to beseech the heavens.

"Here is the church,
the steeple.
Where are the people?"

Maybe learned,
at last,
to make a fist,

or hidden
again
in the dark of their empty hands.

After *Guernica*

we'd seen it and seen it
clearly: Sociopathy and its rationale,

the need of the state, protection racket
that gives the bullies something

to do, something to do without
account, with impunity. Over the door

not the blood of the lamb but the word
WAR: So that now in that house death

is welcome, invited, as in Gaza,
where two men hold a charred corpse,

a child's, for the camera, for our eyes.
Pity? Yes. Horror? Yes.

Who cares what we feel, looking?
We retch at the wretched. Who

are not us. We are troubled
at the breakdown of diplomacy.

Negotiations have broken off.
Yes, right where the child's foot

once was, there, where, like a leg
of lamb, the bone pokes through.

Best Picture

Everyone agreed, it was the greatest movie of the year,
comprised of footage of thousands of separate events
run backward, to a sound track of simple birdsong.

World leaders who had stormed out of meetings
expertly retraced their steps, backward
with a little bounce in contrapuntal rhythm,
to their previous aggressive certainty.

Scene after scene of refugees unloading wagons and trucks,
moving their furniture into their homes, absolutely
certain where each piece, each picture, each utensil, belonged.

Offshore, battleship cannons swallowed round after round
like vacuum tubes debriding an infection. Foot soldiers,
in a flash, stood upright with their legs back under them
and, as if in a children's game, took three giant steps backward.

And, as if from nothing, from nowhere, smoke, fire,
metal, cloth, even blood and flesh converged to become
a busload of people intent on their mundane errands.

Somehow even the scene of the man's sad head
rejoining his slumped shoulders was shot to suggest
a humble gratitude and wasn't in the least grotesque.

And as if the Christians' rapture had arrived,
from the streets of Manhattan, up, up from the sidewalks,
from the crumpled hoods and roofs of cars,
through the clearing air, the people rose, straight up, flying.

Wherever it was shown the people wept and cheered.

2.

Until the whole world went to war at once:
The filmmakers were denounced, reviled
as traitors and propagandists.

"Why didn't they continue going back"
demanded aggrieved historians,
"to when our people suffered?
What about our earlier injury?"

"And ours!" said others.
And ours. And ours. And ours.

Lacrimosa

Behold the Man of Sorrows
on a block of cold stone (broken,
nothing one could use
except to fill in a wall, perhaps,
or mark a boundary) privates
first-class mocking him, a stick
for his sceptre, penetrating
thorns placed artfully, safely
at the scalp line, not what
they'd represent if you looked
with uncommissioned sight.
Soldiers in the emperor's pay?
Of course they did. In uniform,
protecting, for centuries since,
capital, borders, prisons,
reliquaries of that fecal
wooden rod, the ignominious
pike round which a scroll
unlaws the deeds to olive groves,
pastures, fisheries, and homes,
or stands erect, the standard
from which a flag unfurls.

4

An Old Story

A few days after my mother died
the furnace went out, and my father,
who had been sitting in his chair
across from hers since the funeral,

his unshaven chin on his chest,
heaved himself up and went down
the cold gray cellar stairs to see if
he could relight the pilot himself

or would have to call for help.
I know what it must have been like
because I remember him other times
on his back down there, cursing

match after match, god damning
each for burning his fingers, as he
reached through the tiny metal door
as many times as it took. This time

it lit, caught, and roared back to life.
When my father sat up he faced
the washer, the dryer, the empty
laundry basket, the ironing board,

and my mother's radio above the sink,
her absence so vivid that climbing
the stairs he thought he heard her
behind him, and he turned around.

Long Enough

You would have thought it foolish to speak to the dead,
but I have lived two decades longer now than you
and all this time I have carried you in my head

so I think I have the right to question what you said,
dear teacher. My religious upbringing's residue,
you would have thought it foolish. To speak to the dead,

however, is sometimes necessary, especially haunted
by all the things I know you hoped I'd do
with all this time that I have carried you in my head.

In a dream last night I followed where you led
until you asked me in a loud voice what I knew.
(You would have thought it foolish to speak to the dead,

but I was dreaming and could not refuse.) I said
that you were wrong, that I could see your bitter view
(since all this time I have carried you in my head)

for what it was, and you for who you were. Instead
of dreaming your reply I woke as you withdrew.
You would have thought it foolish to speak to the dead
but all this time I have carried you in my head.

Fruit in Season

That spring after my brother's death
I worked in an orchard. Young, good
with a ladder, I pruned apple trees,
lopped crossed limbs, nipped spurs,

and comforted myself with the notion
my brother was busy underground
carefully disentangling the long roots,
season after season, tree by tree;

but now I know there are people
who tread the earth like water
because below them their dead
are trying to grasp their ankles

and pull them under, so I know
how lucky I am and how grateful
I ought to be: Sick for long years,
my brother begrudged me nothing.

Smoke

Does earth have a black box?
In what format? Do we live in it,
characters? At least we could wish
to read our data. But don't we?
This occurs to me, not artwork,
because we're going down.

A morbid anti-metaphysics, like
nearsightedness or subsistence
formalism, never disappoints,
I'll grant myself that; why not?
I'm in the wrong room. I know
because there is no one here I love.

Undercover would be fun,
reporting back, but don't we need
to know what it is we're after?
We can't log everything.
Nobody told you? Me neither.
How about you? You getting paid?

Right now I'm trying to unlearn
metaphor as an opening cognitive
gambit: I can't deal with the alarm!
The reassuring ones are all used up.
Can a mind be tired or are we back
to that beast-of-burden thing?

Beats me. I heard a door slam:
Is it rhetoric? Emphasis? Or prelude
to violence? There's a man takes bets
on things like that. You'd think
someone would stop him, but
by now we all know better.

December 31st

All my undone actions wander
naked across the calendar,

a band of skinny hunter-gatherers,
blown snow scattered here and there,

stumbling toward a future
folded in the New Year I secure

with a pushpin: January's picture
a painting from the 17th century,

a still life: Skull and mirror,
spilled coin purse and a flower.

Hatteras, Sunset

Breakers boom on the sand.
A gull tumbles in a crosswind,

rights himself, then glides
in oblique and waning light.

What does what I want
have to do with anything here?

What is, is, and also its brief
moving shadow, *was.*

What Good

> The fruit,
>
> the red fruit
> that wants to fall—
>
> I am that one.
>
> Sarah Hannah
> "Cicatrix"

I wonder;
are there things I can say
to you now—as if
to you now—I could not

before? After,

there seems more silence,
perhaps

the silence a suicide
imagines, a silence
perfected, as if

requiring the living
speak. But

the amplitude
of that invitation,
the generosity of it,

everyone welcome,

was not yours, friend,
to give. Thief

of a nullity capacious
beyond imagining,

what good does it do us,
I wonder,
to hear its echoing

of a voice, as if
from a well,
as if from the earth,

as if, perhaps,
yours, perfected,

when it is only our own
still failing
to know what to say.

*

Someone says, again, "She took her life,"
and I object. You refused your life.
Am I too harsh? I know I can't know.

But how do I cordon off thoughts
of my two young brothers life refused?
I see them still, in the struggle for breath.

Restraint, I fear, with its many small refusals,
was not for you; the many evenings, one
eye on the weather, putting on your coat

and going home were not for you, nor
the polite excuses; only the one inarguable
and forever private reason you seem to have

had all along. I am trying not to see you
on the sidewalk, lights flashing, yellow
tape, crackling radios. The day I heard,

all I could do was look up at rooftops
and think that something was wrong
with who you thought you were,

or were supposed to be, not who
you were, who you had expertly become.
It left room for argument though,

and argument was what I needed then.
You murdered my colleague, Sarah,
who was becoming my friend,

and you got away with it. And even now
I'm never sure if I am arguing
for the defense or prosecution.

*

 Confusion, fine, of course,
but why like a fond old father
has grief come, opening its arms?

Why are you here, old man?
You're mistaken. Go away.
I didn't know her that well.

*

Where is it written a woman
who throws back her head to laugh,
showing her teeth to the sun with such joy
she has to wipe her eyes
would not, would never?

Where is it written a woman
with a backpack of books
chosen for each of her students,
thumbs hooked through the straps,
humping the weight of their need
on her narrow shoulders
would not, would never?

Where is it written a woman
wise in the ways of pleasure,
quick to jest, to groan at a pun
she could not resist, to suggest

a poet, a film, a restaurant,
would not, could not, would never?

    *

Were there a limbo where
those who were loved
but could not dare
believe it go, then saved
from harm you'd be there,

the door to the roof
locked, on the cold stair,
in a moment's reprieve,
hands in your hair,
still able to conceive,

then, of us, here,
and how sadly we'd move
through irrevocable air,
and it would be enough,
almost, to forestall despair.

    *

Beauty pursued, I hear you:
Better to be the crooked tree,
the bitter, indigestible root,
a berry too tart for even birds,
a pepper too hot, a poison.
Best, if you can, to be no one.
Some say they had noted
like a bulge under your coat,
a pause and a look in your eye,
odd screech in your laugh,
torn cuticle, a strange new way
you moved. Chemicals, neurons,
history—afraid: No one is known,
impressions of presentations,
no one not imagined, myth.
Red fruit fallen in shade.

(I hear you.) No one to blame.
No one in need of forgiveness.

In Hora Mortis Nostrae

1.

To say the day
of my unpersoning
nears is wrong,

as blue sky is
untrue although
a truism,

a prism of gas
and sunlight,
(neuron and word)

"alas" is
an idea
way too small;

2.

better the blue
and beatific
Maria, Mater,

balanced, calm
acrobat atop
all, crushing

the poison snake
in childhood's
dark church,

just the way that
cloud, changing
as the face

of my dying
mother, has nothing
to do with fear.

Instructions

Say I was filled with regret
because I always fell for the future,
and that I learned that hope, like the rain,
can make the wrong things grow.
Explain I would have mourned
much longer if the world had let me.
Say that I hope to be remembered,
and that I wish I had forgotten less.

Set right the rumor I was ever
a believer: A story was told to me
as knowledge and I loved it once,
an arrangement of premises on which
I learned to build all you recall of me.
Belief has nothing to do with faith.
The first I lost early and all at once,
the second later, one loss at a time.

Tell them that, a sailor, I knew fog
was no excuse and certainly no comfort.
Assure them that when I had nothing
to say I said nothing, kept still,
and let things come clear in their time.
Because I spoke clearly does not mean
I remained unlettered, simple, or naïve:
Tell them I saw all there was to see.

Notes

"Ship of Fools" is inspired by Sebastian Brant's *Das Narrenschiff* (1494), a German satirical work that describes 110 assorted follies and vices, with woodcuts mostly by Albrecht Dürer. *Stultifera Navis* (*Ship of Fools*) is the title of the 1497 Latin edition.

"Rising" is for Linda McCarriston.

"after Alciati": Andrea Alciati (sometimes known simply as "Alciato") is the author of *Emblematum Liber* or *The Book of Emblems*, a collection of Latin poems or short prose squibs, first published in 1531. The book was expanded in more than 130 editions during the author's lifetime until it reached its canonical form with 212 emblems. For humanists of the Renaissance, it was as important as the Bible was to the Middle Ages. Based loosely on the epigrams of the Greek Anthology, Alciati's emblems are examples of the Renaissance tradition of "imitations," texts created by adopting the work of another writer, entering into dialogue with it, making use of it as raw material. I have taken that same approach to Alciati's work, aiming to bring the spirit of his *Emblems* to bear on aspects of life that seem to me either immutable or peculiarly contemporary.

   The woodcuts that accompanied the first edition of the *Emblematum* were commissioned by the publisher; in other words, Alciati's writings are not ekphrastic and preceded illustration. Ever since that first edition, however, the *Emblems* have been yoked to the work of visual artists. Alciati's book, known throughout Europe for centuries, spawned a tradition of "emblem poetry" that continued to the end of the 19th century.

   The numbering and ordering of Alciati's *Emblems* is inconsistent across its many editions. I mostly use the numbers as they appear in the online compilation at Memorial University, Newfoundland's, site: www.mun.ca/alciato.

   For all things Alciati I am indebted to John F. Moffitt for *A Book of Emblems: The Emblematum Liber of Andrea Alciati (1492-1550)*, McFarland & Co., Jefferson, NC & London, 2004. Other Alciati materials may be found at www.emblems.arts.gla.ac.uk/alciato and www.studiolum.com/en/cd04.htm

Erato is the Muse of lyric and love poetry.

"Lacrimosa" derives from the "Man of Sorrows" depicted in western liturgical art. I had in mind especially images by Dürer and Gossart.

"Fruit in Season" is in memoriam, Robert James Hoffman, 1950-1972.

"What Good" is in memoriam, Sarah Hannah, 1966-2007, author of *Longing Distance* and *Inflorescence*.

Acknowledgments

I would like to thank the editors of the following periodicals, in which some of these poems, or earlier versions of them, first appeared: *Ascent, Agni, Barrow Street, The Bloomsbury Review, Chautauqua, Cimarron Review, Colorado Review, Ibbetson Street, Janus Head: Journal of Interdisciplinary Studies in Literature, Continental Philosophy, Phenomenological Psychology and the Arts, The Louisville Review, The Ocean State Review, Review Americana,* and *Solstice Literary Magazine.*

"An Old Story" won the 2009 Gretchen Warren Award of the New England Poetry Club.

I would like to express my profound appreciation to The Boston Foundation for a Brother Thomas Fellowship Award, which allowed me to retreat for a time from professional duties to work on several of these poems.

I am grateful to have had the advice and encouragement of fellow poets Kathleen Aguero, Kurt Brown, Richard Cambridge, Robert Gibbons, Jeffrey Harrison, Linda McCarriston, Saul Touster, and Baron Wormser while writing these poems.

I want to thank my editors at Barrow Street Press, poets Peter Covino and Talvikki Ansel especially, for being demanding in the face of my recalcitrance. They have made these poems a better book.

I wish to thank Ellen, Mike, Mikele, Thom, Steve, and Zoya, the "soup group," for the continuing privilege and blessing of your monthly company.

A special thanks to Seymour Slive, Professor of Fine Arts Emeritus, Harvard Museum; former director, Harvard Art Museums, for his enthusiastic support of my Alciati project.

Barrow Street Poetry

Emblem
Richard Hoffman (2011)

Mechanical Fireflies
Doug Ramspeck (2011)

Warranty in Zulu
Matthew Gavin Frank (2010)

Heterotopia
Lesley Wheeler (2010)

This Noisy Egg
Nicole Walker (2010)

Black Leapt In
Chris Forhan (2009)

Boy with Flowers
Ely Shipley (2008)

Gold Star Road
Richard Hoffman (2007)

Hidden Sequel
Stan Sanvel Rubin (2006)

Annus Mirabilis
Sally Ball (2005)

A Hat on the Bed
Christine Scanlon (2004)

Hiatus
Evelyn Reilly (2004)

3.14159+
Lois Hirshkowitz (2004)

Selah
Joshua Corey (2003)